Professor
Janet J. Taylor

How to Examine, Interpret, and Forecast the Thoughts, Emotions, Intentions, and Behaviors of Others

How to Read Minds

Professor Janet J. Taylor

Professor
Janet J. Taylor

Copyright:

Professor
Janet J. Taylor

Acknowledgments

This book, "**How to Read Minds**," is the result of Almighty God's unfailing support, for which I am incredibly grateful. Additionally, my friends' and coworkers' assistance will always be valued.

Professor
Janet J. Taylor

Table of Contents

Professor
Janet J. Taylor

Professor
Janet J. Taylor

INTRODUCTION

Have you ever encountered someone with a natural talent for manipulating other people? To the point where they can frequently predict what other people will say or feel, they seem to have an innate understanding of what makes other people tick and why they behave the way they do. These people can communicate in a way that is truly understood by others, or they can spot deception or manipulation attempts immediately. Occasionally, this kind of individual could be able to interpret the feelings and intentions of others to the extent that it even surpasses their self-awareness. On

Professor
Janet J. Taylor

occasion, it seems like a superpower. In what way do they accomplish this? It's a skill that can be learned and perfected; nothing is particularly magical about it. Some may refer to it as simple social awareness or emotional intelligence. In contrast, others may compare it more to the interview process that a clinical psychologist or psychiatrist uses with a new patient. However, you may think an experienced police officer, private investigator, or FBI agent would acquire this ability over time. We will be closely examining all the methods that we, without a psychology degree or any prior training as a CIA interrogator, might cultivate these skills in ourselves in this book. Undoubtedly, the ability to read and analyze people is a useful one. People are a permanent part of our lives; if we want to live prosperous, peaceful lives, we must collaborate with them. To put it clearly, we may communicate more effectively and gain our desired outcomes when we possess the ability to swiftly and properly assess the

Professor
Janet J. Taylor

character, conduct, and unspoken intentions of others. We can detect deception or influence and modify our communication style to ensure we truly reach our target audience. Those who operate from extremely different values and are very different from us are also easier to understand. The ability to read people is invaluable, whether you're attempting to find out more about someone you just met by looking through their social media account, interviewing a potential new hire, or determining if the mechanic is speaking the truth about your automobile. All of the people you have ever met are mysteries to you. It's absurd. What truly happens in their heads, and how can we know it? What emotions, plans, and thoughts are they harboring? We cannot truly comprehend their actions, the reasons behind their motivations, or even how they perceive and perceive us. We cannot see into the world of another individual. Everything that is not contained within that "black box" is all we have to go

Professor
Janet J. Taylor

on: the things they say, the way they act, the way they seem, the way their voice sounds, their body language, our prior interactions with them, and so forth. The reality that humans are complicated, living, changing organisms with essentially closed inner experiences is important to acknowledge before we go any further in our book. Nobody can truly say with any degree of assurance that they fully understand someone, despite assertions to the contrary from some. Still, there's no doubt that we can improve our ability to interpret the obvious cues. Thinking about other people's cognitive and emotional realities is called having a "theory of mind ."Making a model of someone else's ideas, emotions, and behaviors is a (completely human) desire. It also simplifies the richness and depth of the person before us, just like any model. It doesn't always fully explain reality and has limits like any other model. Developing our ability to assess others more accurately is the aim of our learning process. The

Professor
Janet J. Taylor

skills we acquire involve compiling and intelligently analyzing the most high-quality personal data available. Gaining a more profound comprehension of the individual is possible if we incorporate these little bits of information into one or more reliable and accurate models of human behavior. We may learn to examine live, breathing humans and investigate them to gain a deeper understanding of the what, why, and how of their behavior, much like an engineer can examine a complex mechanism and deduce its intended function. In the upcoming chapters, we will examine various models and differing perspectives on humans, not rival ideas. Utilizing them all at once gives us a new perspective on the individuals in our immediate vicinity. It is our choice what we do with this knowledge. We might apply it to cultivate a more nuanced and sympathetic outlook toward the people we love. Whenever we need to work and collaborate with a wide range of diverse people, we can use our knowledge in the

Professor
Janet J. Taylor

workplace. As parents or love partners, we can apply it to improve ourselves. Improved small talk, the ability to recognize dishonesty or people with ulterior motives, and successful dispute resolution are all possible with it. Perfected sense-making and analytical skills are especially important when we meet someone for the first time. If they interact with others for a sufficient time, even the least socially and emotionally intelligent people can pick up some new skills. In this book, however, we mainly address those abilities that will enable you to obtain genuinely valuable knowledge about people close to you, ideally after just one discussion. Let's take a closer look at developing the skill of accurate, rapid judgment.

Professor
Janet J. Taylor

ONE

The study of interpreting people's behavior and identities

Perception of the mind

Although humans are not able to read the minds of others, they can effectively intuit the thoughts and feelings of others by building mental models. Empathic accuracy is the ability to "read" cues conveyed by another person's words, emotions, and body language. Most people can read others to some extent, but people with mental disorders or those on the autistic spectrum may find it challenging to interpret social signs or emotions in others.

It might be difficult enough to understand our thoughts and motivations, let alone those of strangers, friends, or even relationships. In relationships, a standard critical mental error is overestimating the capacity of a partner or family member to read one's thoughts. This mistake is caused by the assumption that someone who knows someone well should be able to understand one's thoughts and feelings as well, even if they have yet to express them verbally.

Professor
Janet J. Taylor

How Individuals Interpret One Another

Science fiction narratives frequently employ mind reading for evil intent. In the real world, being aware of others' thoughts and feelings enables us to prevent disagreements and misunderstandings while fostering closer bonds.

The most incredible places to start when reading someone's mind—or, more precisely, their mood—are typically through body language, tone, and word choice. Empathy is another essential component: Putting oneself in another person's position can offer important insights into their viewpoint and facilitate a deeper understanding of their ideas, emotions, and behaviors.

Professor
Janet J. Taylor

Physiognomy

The process of determining a person's character or personality from their outward appearance, particularly their face, is known as physiognomy (from the Greek φύσις, 'physis,' meaning "nature" and 'gnomon,' meaning "judge" or "interpreter"). The phrase can also describe the overall appearance of a person, thing, or landscape without mentioning any inferred qualities, such as the countenance of a particular plant or a group of plants.

While the practice of physiognomy is still widely believed in by the general public, it is considered pseudoscience in modern academic circles due to its unsubstantiated claims. However, recent developments in artificial intelligence have reignited interest in the field. The ancient Greek philosophers favored the practice, but it was discredited in the sixteenth century when wanderers and mountain people adopted it. Johann Kaspar Lavater gave it new

Professor
Janet J. Taylor

life and increased its popularity before it lost favor in the late 1800s. In particular, 19th-century physiognomy is cited as the foundation for scientific racism. Modern physiognomy is a topic of increasing scientific interest, particularly regarding facial recognition and machine learning. Today, scientists are primarily concerned with the problems associated with physiognomy in the context of facial recognition algorithms, including privacy concerns.

Sometimes, physiognomy is referred to by the 19th-century word anthroposcopy.

Old

Poetry from the early Greek era occasionally discusses the ancient idea of the correlation between a person's outside and inner nature. Indian Siddhars defined Samudrika Shastra as relating physical attributes to personal traits. Chinese physiognomy,

Professor
Janet J. Taylor

also known as Mian Xiang, is a face-reading technique with at least roots in the Spring and Autumn periods.

Early examples of a developed physiognomic theory can be found in the works of Zopyrus, an expert in the field mentioned in a discussion by Phaedo of Elis in Athens in the fifth century B.C. The philosopher Aristotle often cited theories and writings about the correlation between character and appearance by the fourth century B.C. Aristotle was open to this idea, as this paragraph from his Prior Analytics shows:

If it is granted that the body and the soul are altered simultaneously by the natural affections, it is possible to deduce character from features. However, I say "natural" because, while a man's soul may have changed due to learning music, this is not one of those natural affections; instead, I speak of passions and desires when I speak of natural emotions. We

Professor
Janet J. Taylor

could deduce an animal's character from its features if this were to happen and if each change had a corresponding sign. We could also identify the affection and indication unique to each type of animal.

Translation of Prior Analytics 2.27 by A. J. Jenkinson

Aristotle is credited with writing the first comprehensive physiognomic treatise, Physiognomonica (Physiognomonics), a tiny text most likely the work of his "school" rather than Aristotle himself. The volume is split into two sections, which are assumed to be two distinct works at first. The first portion focuses on human behavior, describes non-Greek races, and explores arguments derived from nature. The second segment divides the animal kingdom into male and female species, concentrating on animal behavior. Correspondences

Professor
Janet J. Taylor

between human form and character can be inferred from these.

The principal surviving physiognomy works after Aristotle are:

- *De Physiognomonia, Polemo of Laodicea (2nd century A.D.), in Greek*
- *Adamantius the Sophist, Greek, Physiognomonica, fourth century*
- *A Latin writer who remains nameless, de Phsiognomonia (ca. 4th century)*

Pythagoras, the Greek mathematician, astronomer, and scientist credited with creating physiognomics, reportedly turned away a potential disciple named Cylon because Pythagoras thought Cylon's appearance suggested he was a terrible man. A physiognomist examined Socrates and declared he was prone to intemperance, sensuality, and violent outbursts of emotion; this was so inconsistent with Socrates's reputation that the physiognomist's students accused him of lying. To resolve the matter, Socrates stated that although he was initially prone to all these vices, he possessed perfect self-control.

Renaissance and Middle Ages

In Middle English, the word "physiognomy" was frequently spelled as "filename" or "victory," as in the fictitious Tale of Beryn, which is part of The Canterbury Tales: "I knowe well by thy fisnamy, thy kind it were to stele."

The validity of physiognomy was formerly widely acknowledged. Early in the 13th century, Michael Scot, a court scholar for Holy Roman Emperor Frederick II, authored a treatise called Liber physiognomiae. Until Henry VIII of England banned "beggars and vagabonds playing 'subtile crafty and unlawful games such as physnomye or 'palmestrye'"

Professor
Janet J. Taylor

in 1530 or 1531, physiognomy was taught in English universities. Around this period, academic elites opposed the notion of 'fisnamy' and adopted the more learned Greek form 'physiognomy.'

In the early sixteenth century, Leonardo da Vinci disregarded physiognomy, calling it "false" and an illusion with "no scientific foundation." Da Vinci thought, however, that the lines on the face that result from expressions on the face can reveal personality qualities. He stated, for instance, that "those who have deep and noticeable lines between the eyebrows are irascible."

Contemporary

Lavater Johann Kaspar

The leading proponent of countenance in the modern era was Johann Kaspar Lavater, a Swiss

Professor
Janet J. Taylor

clergyman who briefly became friends with Goethe (1741–1801). After being initially published in German in 1772, Lavater's works on physiognomy became highly well-known. These crucial writings affected early criminological thought and were translated into French and English.

Professor
Janet J. Taylor

The time frame of renown

Physiognomy's appeal increased throughout the early part of the 18th century and into the 19th. Scholars who were optimistic about its possibilities gave it significant consideration.

Utilize in works of fiction and art.

Numerous European novelists, including Balzac and Chaucer, and portraitists like Joseph Ducreux employed physiognomy to describe their characters. The concept impacted many English writers of the 19th century; this is especially clear from the in-depth physiognomic character descriptions seen in the works of Charles Dickens, Thomas Hardy, and Charlotte Brontë.

Apart from Thomas Browne, two additional writers connected to Norwich who included

Professor
Janet J. Taylor

physiognomical observations in their works are Amelia Opie, a romance novelist, and George Borrow, a travelogue writer.

A fundamental and implicit premise of Oscar Wilde's The Picture of Dorian Gray is physiognomy. In the short stories of Edgar Allan Poe, physiognomy plays a significant role in 19th-century American literature.

Phenotype

Developed about 1800 by German physicians Franz Joseph Gall and Johann Spurzheim, phrenology is a type of physiognomy that measures the bumps on the skull to identify mental and personality qualities. It was trendy in Europe and the United States during the 19th century. The American physician James W. Redfield illustrated the "Resemblances between Men and Animals" with 330

Professor
Janet J. Taylor

engravings in his Comparative Physiognomy, published in 1852. He discovers these in look and (often) character: Jews to Goats, Chinese to Hogs, Blacks to Elephants and Fish, Yankees to Bears, and Germans to Lions.

Phrenology lost credibility and was abandoned when it was linked to countenance in the late 1800s. However, Carl Huter (1861–1912), a German physiognomist, gained popularity in Germany with his "psycho-physiognomy" theory of physiognomy.

Criminal Justice

Sir Francis Galton, an English psychometrician, used composite photography in the late 19th century to try and define physiognomic traits of health, disease, beauty, and criminality. Galton's method involved taking multiple exposures of a face to create a photograph that superimposed two or more faces.

Professor
Janet J. Taylor

He averaged photos of violent offenders and discovered that the resulting composite image seemed "more respectable" than any of the individual faces; this was probably because the final blend averaged out the variations in skin tone across the individual shots. Early in the 1990s, with the development of computer technology, Galton's composite technique was adopted and significantly enhanced with computer graphics software.

Cesare Lombroso, an Italian army doctor and scientist, made efforts to bring physiognomy to the realm of criminology. The idea that "criminality was inherited and that criminals could be identified by physical attributes such as hawk-like noses and bloodshot eyes" was promoted by Lombroso in the middle of the 1800s. Inspired by Charles Darwin's freshly published theories of evolution, Lombroso propagated the use of physiognomy in criminology by bringing many of his misconceptions about evolution to light. The notion that "criminals were

Professor
Janet J. Taylor

'throwbacks' in the phylogenetic tree to early phases of evolution" was the foundation for his reasoning. It is plausible to infer that "according to Lombroso, a regressive characteristic united the genius, the madman and the delinquent; they differed in the intensity of this characteristic and, naturally, in the degree of development of the positive qualities." He believed physical traits alone could determine a person's violent nature. "Lombroso proposed that physical atavistic stigmata, such as the following, could serve as a unique indicator of the "born criminal" based on his findings."

- Massive jaws with a front jaw projection
- A forehead with a low slope
- Prominent cheekbones
- An upside-down or flattened nose
- Ears shaped like handles
- Noses resembling Hawks or plump lips
- Stubbornly shifty eyes
- A sparse beard or becoming bald

Professor
Janet J. Taylor

- Inability to feel pain
- Extended arms in comparison to the legs

This interest in the relationship between criminology and physiognomy began upon Lombroso's first interaction with "a notorious Calabrian thief and arsonist" named Giuseppe Villella. Lombroso was particularly taken by many striking personality characteristics that Villella possessed, agility and cynicism being some of them. Villella's alleged crimes are disputed, and Lombroso's research is seen by many as Northern Italian racism toward Southern Italians. Upon Villella's death, Lombroso "conducted a post-mortem and discovered that his subject had an indentation at the back of his skull, which resembled that found in apes." He later referred to this anomaly as the "median occipital depression." Lombroso used the term "atavism" to describe these primitive, ape-like behaviors that he found in many of those whom he deemed prone to criminality. As he continued analyzing the data he gathered from

Professor
Janet J. Taylor

Villella's autopsy and compared and contrasted those results with previous cases, he inferred that specific physical characteristics allowed for some individuals to have a greater "propensity to offend and were also savage throwbacks to early man."

These examinations yielded far-reaching consequences for various scientific and medical communities at the time. Lombroso wrote, "The natural genesis of crime implied that the criminal personality should be regarded as a particular form of psychiatric disease." This idea is still seen today in psychiatry's diagnostic manual, the DSM-5, in its description of antisocial personality disorder. Furthermore, these ideas promoted the concept that when a crime is committed, it is no longer seen as "free will" but instead a result of one's genetic predisposition to savagery. Lombroso had numerous case studies to corroborate his findings because he was the head of an insane asylum at Pesaro. He was quickly able to study people from various walks of life and was thus able to define criminal types further. Because his theories primarily focused on anatomy and anthropological information, the idea of degeneration being a source of atavism was not explored until later in his criminological theory endeavors. These "new and improved" theories led to the notion "that the born criminal had pathological symptoms in common with the moral imbecile and the epileptic, and this led him to expand his typology to include the insane criminal and the epileptic criminal." In addition, "the insane criminal type [was said to] include the alcoholic, the mattoid, and the hysterical criminal."

The overtly sexist and racist undertones of Lombroso's research have drawn criticism, and the man is still hailed as the father of "scientific criminology" even though many of his theories have been disproven. Lombroso's ideologies are now acknowledged as flawed and regarded as pseudoscience.

Professor
Janet J. Taylor

Modern application

The term "morphopsychology" is a translation of the French word morphopsychologie, which Louis Corman coined in 1937 when he wrote his first book on the subject, Quinze leçons de morphopsychologie (Fifteen Lessons of Morphopsychology). In France, the concept was further developed in the 20th century under the name morphopsychology, produced by Louis Corman (1901–1995), a French psychiatrist who argued that the workings of vital forces within the human body resulted in different facial shapes and forms.

Scientific research

The scientific study or discussion of the relationship between facial features and character has become taboo because of its legacy of racism and

Professor
Janet J. Taylor

junk science passing for criminology. However, there have been many links previously proposed, such as the following: there is evidence that character can influence facial appearance; facial characteristics influence first impressions of others, which in turn influences our expectations and behavior, which in turn influences character; and several biological factors, such as pre-and post-natal hormone levels and gene expression, that influence both facial appearance and character traits.

Deep neural networks (DNNs) are a significant driver of recent advances in artificial intelligence (A.I.) and computer vision. DNNs simulate large, multi-level networks of interconnected neurons, mimicking the structure of the neocortex. DNNs are highly effective at identifying patterns in large amounts of unstructured data, such as digital images, text, or sound, and then analyzing these patterns to make predictions. DNNs' superior performance can help uncover relationships between traits and facial

Professor
Janet J. Taylor

features that the human brain might overlook or misinterpret.

The relationship between facial features and character traits such as political or sexual orientation is complex. Still, it involves the fact that facial features can shape social behavior, partially due to the self-fulfilling prophecy effect. The self-fulfilling prophecy effect asserts that people perceived to have a specific attribute will be treated accordingly and, over time, may engage in behaviors consistent with others' expectations. Conversely, social behavior, such as addictions to drugs or alcohol, can shape facial features. Research in the 1990s indicated that three elements of personality – power, warmth, and honesty – can be reliably inferred by looking at facial features. Some evidence suggested that the pattern of whorls in the scalp had some correlation to male homosexuality, though subsequent research has primarily refuted the findings on hair whorl patterns. A February 2009 article in New Scientist magazine

Professor
Janet J. Taylor

reported that physiognomy is living a minor revival, with research papers trying to find links between personality traits and facial traits. A study of 90 ice hockey players found a statistically significant correlation between a wider face—a greater than average cheekbone-to-cheekbone distance relative to the distance between brow and upper lip—and the number of penalty minutes a player received for violent acts like slashing, elbowing, checking from behind, and fighting.

This resurgence continued in the 2010s with the advent of machine learning for facial recognition; for example, researchers have asserted that merely observing a person's face width can predict certain personality traits (such as a propensity for aggression) and upper body strength. Additionally, political orientation can be reliably predicted; in one study that employed facial recognition technology by examining the faces of over a million participants, political orientation was correctly predicted 74% of

Professor
Janet J. Taylor

the time; this is significantly better than chance (50%), human ability (55%), or even personality questionnaires (68%). Other research has employed A.I. and machine learning techniques to identify facial characteristics that predict intelligence, honesty, and personality.

Researchers, including two A.I. specialists working at Google (one of the two on face recognition), released a supposedly contradicting study in early 2018 based on a survey of 8,000 Americans using Amazon's Mechanical Turk crowd-sourcing platform. The study yielded many traits that were used to discriminate between gay and straight respondents with a series of y-intercepts. In 2017, a controversial study claimed that an A.I. algorithm could detect sexual orientation "more accurately than humans" (in 81% of the tested cases for men and 71% for women). A director of research at the Human Rights Campaign (HRC) accused the study of being "junk science" to the BBC. The researchers criticized the director, an

Professor
Janet J. Taylor

"equity and inclusion strategist" with no scientific background, for "premature judgment."

While most of the facial images' predictive power is attributable to basic demographics (age, Gender, race) extracted from the face, image artifacts, observable facial characteristics, and other image features extracted by deep learning all contribute to prediction quality beyond demographics, a 2020 study on the use of consumer facial images for marketing research purposes concluded that deep learning on facial images could extract a variety of personal information relevant to marketers and so users' facial photos could become a basis for ad targeting on Tinder and Facebook.

Professor
Janet J. Taylor

Personality: What Is It?

The term personality refers to the long-lasting traits and behaviors that make up an individual's distinct way of adjusting to life; these include significant characteristics, interests, drives, values, self-concept, abilities, and emotional patterns. The field of personality psychology studies the nature and definition of personality and its development, structure, and trait constructs, dynamic processes, variations (with an emphasis on enduring and stable individual differences), and maladaptive forms. Different theories explain the structure and development of personality in various ways, but all agree that personality influences behavior.

Understanding these personality types, often Type A, B, C, and D, sheds light on how we approach challenges, communicate, and make choices. Our personalities act as the architects and artists of our lives, influencing our reactions to experiences and the

Professor
Janet J. Taylor

outcomes we achieve. A person's personality is the lens through which they perceive the world, shaping their thoughts, behaviors, and interactions.

If you understand these personality types, they aid in self-discovery and personal development. It is a bridge to improved empathy and communication and helps gain a deeper appreciation for the unique qualities in people. Over many decades, numerous psychologists, researchers, and enthusiasts have studied and refined the concept of personality types. And while no single framework captures the full complexity of the human character, these four distinct personality types offer valuable insights into our core tendencies and preferences.

Professor
Janet J. Taylor

The Four Fundamental Temperaments

The four personality types date back more than two millennia to ancient Greece when Hippocrates named the temperaments choleric, melancholic, phlegmatic, and sanguine after bodily fluids. These temperaments were supposedly derived from the humoral medicine theory and have endured through various historical interpretations and modifications.

1. Choleric

The choleric temperament is associated with an excess of yellow bile, one of the four humors. Cholerics are extroverted, driven by a desire for control and power, and are regarded as assertive, competitive, and ambitious. They are natural leaders who are frequently quick to make decisions and take charge of situations.

Professor
Janet J. Taylor

2. Depressing

Melancholics are considered introverted, thoughtful, analytical, deep thinkers, and compassionate people prone to introspection and self-analysis. They are also linked to artistic and creative tendencies. The melancholic temperament is associated with an excess of black bile.

3. Phlegmatic

The phlegmatic temperament is associated with excess phlegm, another bodily fluid. People with a phlegmatic temperament are described as stable, patient, good-natured, peaceful, and prefer to avoid conflict and maintain harmony in their surroundings.

Professor
Janet J. Taylor

4. Sanguine

Sanguines are thought to be optimistic and lively people who approach life with enthusiasm. The sanguine temperament is associated with an excess of blood. People with a sanguine temperament are considered outgoing, social, and cheerful. They are frequently perceived as extroverts who enjoy socializing and are quick to make friends.

Professor
Janet J. Taylor

Types of personalities

The ABCD personality type was first described in the 1950s by two cardiologists, Meyer Friedman and Ray Rosenman. Initially, it only included Type A and Type B personalities; later, it also included Type C and Type D personalities. The four personality types classify people based on behavior, attitudes, and stress responses.

Many labels and titles have been applied to these four personality types: Type A, B, C, and D personalities. Every person is a combination of these four personality types.

- ## Typical A personality

In essence, Type A personalities are driven but can also appear aggressive. Type A(s) are inspiring and dependable individuals who push boundaries and venture outside their comfort zone. They have high standards and are fiercely competitive. Individuals with type A personalities are perfectionists and goal-oriented. They are also prone to stress, impatience, and a sense of time urgency.

At work, type A personalities are distinguished by their strong delegation and administrative abilities; they like to operate autonomously and establish their schedules; they also exhibit productivity and valuable problem-solving skills.

- **Personality type B**

A type B personality is laid back, easygoing, patient, creative, imaginative, and less likely to experience stress. Type B personalities are grounded and peaceful and make people feel at ease; people enjoy being around them. They are compassionate, wise, and understand how to be there for others and themselves.

Professor
Janet J. Taylor

At work, type B personalities are gregarious, enthusiastic, and outgoing. They enjoy working in groups and are excellent in client relations. They flourish in cooperative settings.

- **Personality types: Type A vs Type B**

A team with a mix of Type A and Type B personalities works well because Type A personalities help the team stay on track, and Type B personalities build good relationships. While Type B people often get their motivation from others, Type A people remain motivated independently. Understanding both personality types is vital to ensure the team works well together. Type A and Type B personalities are two different personality styles. Type A personalities like to plan for the future and are focused on goals. Type B personalities are more laid back and care about getting along with others in the present.

Professor
Janet J. Taylor

- **Personality type C**

Individuals with a Type C personality are analytical, meticulous, and accuracy-driven. They are prone to experiencing emotional strain. Type C personalities are reserved and introverted in social situations. They enjoy routines, prefer a fixed life, and crave logic, order, and precision.

Because it helps them prioritize things and see them through to completion, type C personalities enjoy clearly defined job roles and expectations. At work, they are logical, prepared, and outcome-driven.

Professor
Janet J. Taylor

- **Personality type D**

The Type D personality type is characterized by introversion, holding their emotions close to the vest, sensitivity, lack of optimism, a need for security, resilience, sage guidance, and a persistent attitude.

At work, type D personalities are organized, task-oriented, driven by consistency and routine, well-organized, and frequently prefer a relaxed environment.

- **Personality type X**

Type Xs are often identified as Type Ax/Bx, where 'x' denotes the intersection between two distinct personality types. Type Xs possess many personalities, each in equal ratio to the other.

Professor
Janet J. Taylor

A subset of individuals possessing four balanced personality types are called Type X personalities because they adapt to changing situations.

Professor
Janet J. Taylor

Additional ideas and characteristics of personality

Personality types can be broadly classified into four types or over sixteen combinations. In modern psychology, the study of personality has evolved significantly, with various models and theories providing an evidence-based understanding of human personality. The historical concept of the four basic temperaments remains a critical part of the history of psychology and personality theory.

Other personality models, like the Big Five, also known as the Five Factor Model, focus on five broad dimensions of personality: openness, conscientiousness, extraversion, agreeableness, and neuroticism (OCEAN). Personality type models vary in their approaches, but one well-known system that uses four personality dimensions is the Myers-Briggs Type Indicator (MBTI). MBTI categorizes individuals into sixteen personality types based on four aspects:

Professor
Janet J. Taylor

extraversion/introversion, sensing/intuition, thinking/Feeling, and judging/perceiving.

It is difficult to identify different personality types, but it is possible to recognize changes in personality types over time. Personality is complex and influenced by various factors, including genetics, upbringing, and life experiences. Each personality type brings its unique characteristics and tendencies to the forefront, shedding light on how individuals navigate the complexities of life, work, and relationships.

In the end, recognizing and embracing the subtleties of personality types builds more robust and inclusive communities. A solid understanding of these personality types is a valuable self-awareness tool that enables individuals to recognize their strengths and weaknesses. It also helps appreciate the diversity of human nature, foster empathy, and

Professor
Janet J. Taylor

facilitate effective communication. Personality tests can be used for growth and self-reflection.

Professor
Janet J. Taylor

Can your personality type change? Are personalities fixed?

People change. The fact that you witness people's changes in your personal and professional lives has led some to question the foundation of personality type theory. If people change over time, is there a consistent personality type that applies to a person's life? The answer may seem contradictory, but personality type does not change with a person's personality.

Depending on the definition, "personality" can mean anything from "the total of the physical, mental, emotional, and social characteristics" to "the organized pattern of behavioral characteristics of the individual." These broad definitions undoubtedly include aspects of people who do change over time. "Personality type," on the other hand, has a more precise definition based on whether an individual naturally prefers:

- Introversion/Extraversion (I/E)
- Sensing/Intuition (S/N)
- Thinking/Feeling (T/F)
- Judging/Perceiving (J/P)

These four preferences make up an individual's MBTI personality type, which the theory states is stable over time. To understand how people can change while their underlying personality preferences stay stable, let's look at two significant situations where people frequently exhibit notable signs of change: adjusting to new work realities and seeking new career challenges.

Professor
Janet J. Taylor

Learning from experience and making adjustments

Suppose you are more inclined toward Thinking (T) than Feeling (F). In that case, you typically base your decisions on your analysis of the logical consequences and make an effort to mentally distance yourself from the decision to weigh the pros and cons. Personal values, empathy, and the effects of those decisions on others—qualities essential to someone with a Feeling preference—become secondary considerations. That being said, you can still learn empathy as a skill to enhance your capacity in that area. For example, if a chief operations officer decides to switch suppliers, they probably did so based on anal.

Imagine, however, that the COO had also learned from experience or leadership training that such drastic changes could have a less evident, but no less natural, effect on morale, retention, etc., and that this blowback can hurt the company; if the officer takes this into account in their handling of the situation, perhaps by adopting a much more personal approach to ease employees' emotions, then they have demonstrated change.

That leader may have acquired the capacity to transcend their personality type and adapt to the demands of the circumstance, even though taking care of such matters may not come naturally to them (a process known as "flexing their preferences").

Have they altered?

Yes, and in this instance, in a positive way.

However, what specifics have changed?

It indicates that the person has developed perspective and adaptability and learned to use their non-dominant preference for Feeling. The fact that they have learned to think and behave differently does not imply that the tendency to conform to their more comfortable and familiar Thinking preference isn't still present or that it would be an easier and more relaxed route.

Professor
Janet J. Taylor

Seeking out fresh challenges

People change for various reasons, including necessity and experience. Still, people can also change because they want to grow beyond who they have always been; this is especially true in the case of careers, where a person may decide to learn software coding after spending their entire adult life in creative design because they find the old way of doing things to be too easy.

- Have they undergone a profound change in personality type?
- The fundamental personality preferences remain unchanged.

However, their line of work has enabled them to utilize and develop their innate empathy and harmony-seeking tendencies fully. In that case, they might eventually feel compelled to address the less developed aspect of their nature by learning to solve

Professor
Janet J. Taylor

problems analytically, logically, and with cause-and-effect reasoning.

While actions and personalities can fluctuate, personality type is constant.

Professor
Janet J. Taylor

How to Determine Your Personality (Accurately)

After learning that many tests must be validated and reliable, you may wonder if there's an accurate way to measure personality. Well, readers, the answer is yes! In the last two posts of this series, I'll talk about a model of personality that has been validated by science and explain why it performs better than the MBTI and Enneagram.

What Constitutes the Big Five?

The "Big Five" personality traits—extraversion, agreeableness, conscientiousness, emotional stability, and openness to experience—represent five categories of individual qualities that tend to cluster together in persons and are measured by most personality psychologists using these tests.

Professor
Janet J. Taylor

You are probably familiar with the terms "extraversion," "introversion," or the more recent term that has become common usage, "ambivert." Many people associate extraversion only with sociability, but extraversion includes many more traits, such as assertiveness, activity level, cheerfulness, and excitement-seeking, all of which strongly correlate.

Individuals with high openness to trying new things have various interests and are curious, adventurous, intellectual, and imaginative. Five-Factor Theory and Social Investment Theory explain the complex processes by which our genes, experiences with others, investment in relationships and institutions, environments, culture, life events, and self-reflections interact to shape our unique mixture of these five traits. Agreeableness is a person's tendency to be trusting, kind, cooperative, sympathetic, humble, and generous. Conscientious people are persistent, hard-working, self-controlled, responsible, and organized.

These characteristics characterize your general consistent patterns of thoughts, feelings, and behaviors. You may have noticed that you sometimes seem a little different depending on the circumstance or the person; this is because there are situations in which we are required to act in ways that are not consistent with our natural tendencies. For instance, my students are usually surprised to learn that I consider myself to be somewhat introverted; in class, I am gregarious, lively, animated, and excited.

"I'm not an extravert, but I play one on T.V.," I tell them. Although I am genuinely excited to discuss psychology with my students, I might be less energy-expending if I had my choice because it takes a lot of energy to be as pleasant as they need me to connect with them. Even though my behavior varies a little bit depending on the circumstance, I will still be less

Professor
Janet J. Taylor

extroverted on average than someone who is genuinely more extroverted than I am.

Professor
Janet J. Taylor

How Are the Big Five Organized?

Most people fall somewhere between the two extremes as the Big Five are relatively generally distributed in the population. Some people use the term "ambivert" to describe someone who is neither totally introverted nor highly extroverted. However, an ambivert is someone who, like many people, has moderate extraversion! These five traits are measured separately, on a continuum from low to high, and your score on each trait could be at the very bottom, the very top, or anywhere in between!

Many Big Five questionnaires measure the five facets, or the sub-components of the Big Five traits, and the main characteristics; this allows for a more nuanced and personalized measurement. For example, a scale that measures extraversion at the facet level might give you a score on sociability, assertiveness, activity, cheerfulness, and excitement-seeking.

Professor
Janet J. Taylor

If you are moderately extraverted, it could mean that you are somewhere in the middle on each of its facets, or you are high on some and low on others, but the average across them is in the middle. It also helps you understand why you scored as having moderate levels of a trait.

For example, I am on the lower side of moderate extraversion because I tend to be reserved and have low energy and activity levels, but I'm pretty assertive and cheerful. Similarly, when it comes to conscientiousness, I score on the higher end of moderate because I am self-controlled, responsible, and productive. Still, I beg you not to go to my house or office lest my lack of orderliness shatters any illusion you might have of my high conscientiousness. But just because I'm relatively high on conscientiousness, it doesn't mean that I will necessarily score highly on any of the other traits. The Big Five are independent of one another, meaning your score on one trait does not influence your level

Professor
Janet J. Taylor

of another trait. Being reserved (low extraversion) does not mean that someone must also be self-conscious (low emotional stability), although you probably know people who are. Similarly, being achievement-oriented and self-disciplined (high conscientiousness) does not mean by default that you are intellectually curious (high openness to experience), although you may be.

Research has shown that we tend to like people who are high in openness to experience much more than low people, and the same is valid to a lesser extent for conscientiousness and agreeableness. Although there are not huge differences in how much we like people at opposite ends of the extraversion spectrum, individually, you may get some unflattering results: some people are aloof, lazy, neurotic, closed-minded jerks. However, different cultures or even subcultures tend to value or reward certain levels of these traits over others.

Professor
Janet J. Taylor

67

Professor
Janet J. Taylor

TWO

Overview of Interpreting Body Language

The nonverbal cues we employ to communicate are called body language. Many of these nonverbal cues are used in everyday communication. Body language could comprise as much as 60% to 65% of communication. Facial emotions, eye contact, gestures, posture, and bodily movements are a few examples of body

Professor
Janet J. Taylor

language. The things we choose not to say can often reveal much information.

What makes body language significant, then? Understanding oneself and others through body language is possible. It gives us insight into the potential emotions of individuals in a particular circumstance. Additionally, body language can be used to convey intents or feelings. Although gestures, eye contact, and facial emotions are frequently recognized as the three main categories of body language, other elements like posture and physical proximity can also be utilized to transmit messages. While interpreting body language is crucial, it's also critical to be aware of other indicators, like context. Instead of concentrating on a single action, you should frequently consider signals as a collection.

This book explores the functions of body language in communication and provides examples

Professor
Janet J. Taylor

and explanations of various body language expressions.

Professor
Janet J. Taylor

Expressions on the Face

Please take a moment to consider how much can be said about someone by simply observing their facial expressions. A grin can convey satisfaction or acceptance. A frown can convey displeasure or disapproval. Our facial expressions can sometimes express how we feel about a particular circumstance. Even though you claim to be feeling good, the expression on your face can suggest otherwise.

A few instances of emotions that can be conveyed through facial expressions are as follows:

- Contentment
- Depressing
- Fury
- Unexpected
- Disgust
- A fear
- Perplexity
- Joy
- A wish

Professor
Janet J. Taylor

- Disdain

Even our level of trust or belief in someone's words can be gauged by their facial expression.

Psychologists have found a lot of fascinating things regarding body language. One study discovered that a slight smile plus a small lift of the eyebrows constituted the most reliable facial emotion. The researchers hypothesized that this look exudes confidence and warmth. One of the most common types of body language is facial expression. Around the world, there are common phrases for melancholy, happiness, wrath, and fear.

The universality of a range of facial expressions associated with specific emotions, including happiness, anger, fear, surprise, and sadness, has been supported by research by Paul Ekman. Research suggests we infer someone's I.Q. from their expressions and countenances.

Professor
Janet J. Taylor

One study indicated that those with narrower faces and more prominent noses were more likely to be evaluated as intelligent. People with smiling, joyous expressions were also considered more intellectual than those with furious looks.

The Eyes

The eyes are often called the "windows to the soul" because they can reveal much about a person's thoughts and feelings. Observing another person's eye movements throughout a discussion is a natural and crucial aspect of communication.

Typical observations include whether or not someone is looking directly into your eyes, how quickly they blink, and whether or not their pupils are dilated. Paying attention is the best approach to decipher someone's body language. Keep an eye out for any of these eye signs.

Professor
Janet J. Taylor

Gaze with the eyes

During a conversation, it shows that someone is interested and paying attention when they look you in the eyes. Prolonged eye contact, nevertheless, can appear dangerous. However, if someone constantly averts their gaze and breaks eye contact, it could be a sign that they are uncomfortable, distracted, or trying to hide their genuine emotions.

Squinting

Although it's normal for someone to blink, you should also notice whether they blink too little or too much. When someone is upset or uneasy, they frequently blink more quickly. A person who blinks seldom may be making a conscious effort to control their eye movements. For instance, a poker player

Professor
Janet J. Taylor

may deliberately try to look unimpressed with the hand he was dealt by blinking less often.

- **Student Volume**

One very subtle nonverbal communication indication is pupil size. Environmental light levels regulate pupil dilation, although emotions can also occasionally lead to slight variations in pupil size. For instance, you've probably heard the expression "bedroom eyes" used to characterize the glance a person delivers to someone they find attractive. For example, noticeably dilated eyes can convey curiosity or even arousal.

Professor
Janet J. Taylor

The Oral Organ

Understanding mouth gestures and expressions is very crucial when interpreting body language. For instance, chewing on the bottom lip could be a sign of anxiety, fear, or insecurity in the person. If someone is coughing or yawning, covering their Mouth could be an attempt at politeness, but it could also be an attempt to hide a disapproving scowl.

While smiling is undoubtedly one of the most effective body language expressions, there are numerous interpretations of smiles. A smile can convey sincerity or be employed to convey cynicism, sarcasm, or even false delight.

The following mouth and lip signals should be noted while analyzing body language:

- **Pursed lips:** Squeezing your lips together could signify dislike, disapproval, or mistrust.

Professor
Janet J. Taylor

- **Lip biting:** When under stress, worry, or anxiety, people occasionally bite their lips.
- **Mouth covering:** People may cover their mouths to avoid grinning or smirking when they wish to conceal an emotional response.
- **Turned up or down:** Minor alterations in the Mouth can often serve as imperceptible clues about an individual's emotional state. It could indicate happiness or optimism when the Mouth is slightly turned up. Conversely, a somewhat pulled-down mouth can convey feelings of melancholy, Disgust, or even a scowl.

Motions

Among the most straightforward forms of body language communication are gestures. Joint and easily comprehensible motions to communicate numerical amounts are waving, pointing, and using fingers. However, some gestures may be cultural, so

Professor
Janet J. Taylor

in another nation, giving the thumbs up or making the peace sign may imply something entirely different than it does in the U.S.

A few instances of famous gestures and their potential meanings are as follows:

- **A closed fist** can convey camaraderie in some circumstances or rage in others.
- **Giving someone the thumbs up or down** indicates acceptance or displeasure.
- **The "okay" gesture** can be defined as extending the other three fingers while making a circle with the thumb and index finger to indicate "okay" or "all right." In some parts of Europe, on the other hand, the same signal is used to suggest you are nothing. In several nations in South America, the symbol is genuinely a crude motion.
- In many cultures, **the V sign**—made by raising the index and middle fingers and separating

Professor
Janet J. Taylor

them to form a V—means victory or peace. When the back of the hand is pointing outward, the gesture acquires an offensive connotation in the U.K. and Australia.

The limbs

Nonverbal cues can also be sent with the arms and legs. Arms crossed might be interpreted as defensive. Moving your legs apart from someone else could signify distaste or unease. Keeping the arms close to the body may be an attempt to reduce oneself or attract attention away from oneself. In contrast, other subtle signals, like spreading the arms widely, may be an attempt to seem more prominent or more commanding.

When assessing nonverbal cues, be mindful of the following indications that the arms and legs may display:

Professor
Janet J. Taylor

- Crossed arms may indicate defensiveness, self-preservation, or closedness.
- Placing hands on hips when standing can either be a sign of aggression or of someone who is poised and in control.
- Placing hands behind the back could signify boredom, nervousness, or even rage.
- Fidgeting or tapping fingers quickly can indicate boredom, impatience, or frustration.
- Crossed legs may indicate needing privacy or feeling locked off.

Position

A key component of body language is how we hold our bodies. How we hold our bodies and a person's overall physical appearance are considered aspects of posture. A person's posture can reveal much about

Professor
Janet J. Taylor

their emotional state and subtle aspects of their personality, such as confidence level, openness, or submissiveness. For example, sitting up straight may show that someone is concentrated and aware of what is happening, and conversely, hunching over when sitting could suggest that a person is uninterested or uncaring.

Pay attention to some indications that a person's posture can convey when attempting to read body language.

- Maintaining an open and exposed trunk is critical to open posture. Posing in this way conveys warmth, willingness, and openness.
- Closed posture is when the torso is hidden, usually by bending forward and crossing the arms and legs. Anxiety, hostility, and hatred can all be indicated by this kind of stance.

Professor
Janet J. Taylor

Individual Space

Have you ever heard someone talk about how they need their own space? When someone gets a bit too near to you, have you ever started to feel uneasy?

Anthropologist Edward T. Hall first used the term "proxemics" to describe the space that separates people when they engage. The physical space between people can convey much nonverbal information, just as body language and facial emotions.

- **Close Range: 6 to 18 Inches**

This degree of physical separation frequently denotes a closer bond or more comfort between people. Usually, it happens during close bodily contact, like touching, speaking, or hugging.

Professor
Janet J. Taylor

- **Individual Length: 1.5 to 4 feet**

This degree of physical separation typically occurs between close friends or family members. The degree of closeness in a relationship can be inferred by how close two individuals can stand to each other while interacting.

- **4 to 12 feet is the social distance.**

This degree of physical separation is frequently employed when interacting with acquaintances. You may feel more at ease engaging at a closer distance with someone you know reasonably well, such as a coworker you see multiple times a week.

A distance of ten to twelve feet could feel more comfortable when you don't know the other person well, like when you encounter a postal delivery driver once a month.

Professor
Janet J. Taylor

- **Distance to Public: 12 to 25 ft**

This kind of physical separation is frequently employed in public speaking scenarios. Two of these circumstances are giving a presentation at work or speaking in front of a large class of pupils. It's also critical to remember that different cultures may require different amounts of personal space for people to feel at ease.

One frequently given example is the distinction between individuals from Latin America and those from North America. When interacting, people from Latin America like to stand closer to one another, but people from North America require more personal space.

Professor
Janet J. Taylor

Nonverbal Communication's Functions

In social interactions, body language is essential in many ways. It can aid in making the following possible:

1. **Gaining trust:** This can be accomplished by making eye contact, nodding in agreement while listening, or even unintentionally copying the other person's body language.

2. **Point emphasis:** How you speak, interact with others by using hand and arm movements, and occupy space all impact how your message is received.13

3. **Exposing realities:** We may be able to tell whether someone is lying or not being completely honest about their feelings based on their body language rather than just what they say.

Professor
Janet J. Taylor

4. **Being aware of your needs:** Our bodies communicate much about our emotions. Are you, for example, hunching over, clenching your jaw, or pursed lips? It could indicate that you're being triggered by something in your current surroundings. Your body may be alerting you to feelings of anxiety, fear, or any other combination of emotions.

But remember that you might only sometimes interpret someone else's body language accurately.

What can you learn about a person from their body language?

You may infer any emotion from someone's body language, including anxiety, anger, and excitement. Moreover, it could allude to personality qualities (e.g., an individual's shyness or extroversion). However, body language is deceptive. It depends on a person's mind, degree of energy, and Environment.

Professor
Janet J. Taylor

Sometimes, a person lacks eye contact, which is a sign of untrustworthiness, but it doesn't always follow that you can't trust someone who isn't making eye contact with you. They may be preoccupied and thinking of something else. Alternatively, there might be a cultural disparity at work.

How to Communicate More Effectively Without Words

Paying attention is the first step towards developing your nonverbal communication skills. See if you can sense your body language and that of others.

You may look at the ground when someone is telling you a story. Instead, you could make eye contact and even crack a small smile to convey your interest and attention.

Professor
Janet J. Taylor

What constitutes appropriate body language?

Positive body language, sometimes referred to as good body language, is the expression of enthusiasm and interest. It can be achieved, among other things, by listening with an open and straight posture, maintaining eye contact, grinning, and nodding.

Finding balance is crucial in communicating with intention through body language. For example, a firm handshake might demonstrate professionalism before a job interview. However, if you grip it too tightly, the other person might get hurt or uncomfortable. Remember to take other people's feelings into account. Furthermore, keep refining your emotional intelligence. It's usually easier to sense how others feel about you when you're more aware of your feelings. When someone is receptive and open, or when they are closed off and need space, you will be able to tell.

Professor
Janet J. Taylor

We can take advantage of our body language to feel the way we want to feel. For example, research found that people who maintained an upright seated posture while dealing with stress had higher levels of self-esteem and more positive moods than those with a slumped posture.

Professor
Janet J. Taylor

THREE

How to Recognize and Interact with Introverts

What's an Introvert?

An introvert is a person who possesses traits associated with the introverted personality type, meaning that they

Professor
Janet J. Taylor

prefer to concentrate on their inner ideas and thoughts as opposed to what is going on outside of themselves. Rather than being in big groups or crowds, they prefer to spend time with just one or two people.

The term introvert may conjure images of a quiet, reserved person who enjoys solitude. There's much more to introverts than that, although that may be true for some. How you interpret the Environment around you determines whether you are an extrovert or an introvert. In the 1920s, a psychologist named Carl Jung coined introvert and extrovert, frequently spelled extravert. Those with these two personality types are categorized according to how they obtain and use energy. According to Jung, extroverts look to other people to meet their energy demands, whereas introverts use their brains to refuel.

Professor
Janet J. Taylor

Indices That May Point to an Introvert

Introverts make up between one-third and half of the population in the United States. Even if their appearance varies, introverts exhibit many of the same behavioral characteristics. Generally speaking, introverts have the following traits:

- Need quiet to concentrate
- Are reflective
- Are self-aware
- Take time to make decisions
- Feel comfortable being alone
- Don't like group work
- I prefer to write rather than talk
- Feel exhausted after being in a crowd
- I have few, but I am close to these friends
- Daydream or use their imaginations to solve problems. Retreat into their minds to rest.

Professor
Janet J. Taylor

A test like the Myers-Briggs Type Indicator (MBTI), the SAPA project, or the Big Five approach described in Chapter 2 (How to Measure Your Personality Accurately) can all be used to determine your introverted tendencies.

Professor
Janet J. Taylor

Reasons for Being Introverted

The exact reason for introversion versus extroversion is unknown to scientists. They are aware that the two personality types' brains function somewhat differently. Researchers have discovered that introverts have more blood flowing to their frontal lobes than extroverts. This area of the brain aids in planning, problem-solving, and memory. Additionally, introverted brains process dopamine in a different way than extroverted brains. That's the chemical that activates your brain's reward and pleasure centers. The chemical content of introverted and extroverted brains is identical, but the reward area in extroverts' brains experiences an exciting buzz. Conversely, introverts usually feel exhausted by it.

Professor
Janet J. Taylor

Different Types of Introverts

Being an introvert doesn't mean you have to accept it. According to psychologists, introverts are somewhere along a spectrum. A person's introversion varies from person to person. Some people's positions are precisely in the middle. We refer to them as ambiverts. Both introverts and extroverted people typically have some extroverted traits mixed in with their introverted ones. Being an introvert can manifest itself in many different ways.

According to one study, introverts typically fit into one of four subtypes:

1. Social introverts: This is the "classic" introvert type. Social introverts prefer peaceful environments and small gatherings to large crowds.

Professor
Janet J. Taylor

2. Thinking introverts: This subgroup consists of daydreamers. They have vivid imaginations and are often lost in their thoughts.

3. Anxious introverts: Besides wanting time alone, these people also seek out alone since they frequently experience social anxiety or shyness.

4. Restricted or inhibited introverts: These individuals deliberate before acting. They are not going to decide on the spur of the moment. They typically take longer to act.

You might become less introverted over time and in specific contexts. It's unlikely that you will suddenly become more outgoing. But depending on what's going on in your life, you might become more or less introverted.

Professor
Janet J. Taylor

Shyness versus introversion

Though the two are unrelated, introverts are sometimes mistaken for shy persons. Although shyness is an emotion, introversion is a personality type. Shy people sometimes feel awkward or uneasy in social settings, mainly among strangers. They can start sweating because they are so anxious. They can have a stomachache and feel their heart beat more quickly. They might be more likely to avoid social gatherings if they dislike the unpleasant emotions that consume their bodies and minds when required to attend parties or other events.

Although introverted people avoid social gatherings, they find it more energizing or comfortable to do things alone or with a small group. Introverts prefer to be alone or in small groups; they don't skip social occasions since, unlike shy people, they respond negatively to more significant gatherings.

Professor
Janet J. Taylor

Myths Concerning Introverts

It's a frequent misconception that introverts are timid people. While some introverts might be bashful, this isn't always the case. Other misconceptions consist of:

- It doesn't matter how gregarious you are—being an introvert doesn't make you less friendly. Introverts may be perceived as being hostile since they don't usually hang out with big groups of people and prefer to think things through in private rather than participate in group discussions.

- Introverts cannot be leaders: While extroverted personalities are typically associated with leaders, introverts can be bosses and leaders. They can keep focused on long-term objectives, listen to the opinions of their staff, and seem less intimidating, which helps them be accepted in their positions. These are some of the traits that make them good leaders.

- Getting to know introverts can be challenging, as they tend to form close friendships with a limited number of individuals. Even though they might not be approachable to everyone who wants to initiate a conversation, those close to them get to know them well and become true friends.

Professor
Janet J. Taylor

Advice on Interacting with Introverts

1. Engage in active listening

Extroverts naturally enjoy active listening. However, introverts and extroverts differ slightly in this regard. While introverts prefer your curiosity, extroverts prefer your attention. They enjoy having their needs met. For an introvert, nodding your head, leaning in, and taking notes when necessary are all excellent indications that you are actively listening.

2. Consider your words before speaking

We've already advised introverts to accommodate extroverts who want to discuss things aloud, but occasionally, it can assist if extroverts meet introverts halfway. If that's not possible, let them know you're

Professor
Janet J. Taylor

thinking aloud so they may pay closer attention to your findings rather than your methodology.

3. Honor the need for privacy

Privacy is more important than secrecy, particularly regarding personal information. Open workplaces make extroverts feel more at ease, but introverts may be more uncomfortable. Invite the introvert to a location where you are less likely to be overheard if you are going to have a private talk. If you do this, they will interact with you more thoroughly.

4. Speak quietly and slowly

Though not sluggish, introverts do require time to think things through. Consider the distinction between eating with flavor and consuming it quickly. Introverts cherish conversations. They enjoy pauses

Professor
Janet J. Taylor

between statements because it allows them to savor the aftertaste. It's common to "see" them pondering during those moments. When they make a valuable contribution to the discourse, the wait will be worthwhile.

5. Pick a distraction-free time and location for your communication

There's a reason why they're called distractions. Introverts prefer to avoid having their attention divided between several places simultaneously, but extroverts do. Additionally, because they prefer to focus on just one topic at a time, they are particularly bothered by distractions.

Professor
Janet J. Taylor

6. Hold off and await a reply

An expansion of the advice is in point four above. It's a common belief that the spaces between notes create music. For introverts, the discussion is made up of the spaces between phrases. They may interpret the comments and run them through their database to make sense of everything.

7. Avoid appearing overbearing or insistent on an answer right away

Pausing is something that introverts enjoy; it gives them time to reflect. After hearing what you say, they leave and interpret it for themselves. With this processing period, it can be easier for them to reach a choice or an opinion if one is needed. But this does not imply that it may be left open-ended. Agree on when they will get back to you and find out if they

Professor
Janet J. Taylor

need time to consider it. Undoubtedly, the wait will be worthwhile.

8. Give details and schedule processing time ahead of time

An agenda or a few talking points ahead of time will assist the introvert in preparing for the conversation by considering their need for processing time. Additionally, if you are in a meeting and want input from everyone there, start with the extroverts, who are more willing to do so than the introverts.

9. Stay on topic

First, Subject. When. A. Time. Diverse topics are more comfortable for extroverts since they enjoy variety. Since introverts enjoy depth, they prefer to go further into each subject before moving on. By comparing

Professor
Janet J. Taylor

them to tango and jitterbug, you may understand the depth and attention that introverts prefer over extroverts.

10. Condense your final thoughts and the course of action that you have decided upon

It is valid for both introverts and extroverts and serves as confirmation for the latter. Frequently, the summary will highlight something they just "forgot" to mention or an assumption they had made that the other person had missed. Make it obvious who is expected to do what and when.

Professor
Janet J. Taylor

FOUR

How to recognize extroverts and interact with them

Do you like interacting socially with people outside of your immediate circle? Do you get excited about the prospect of meeting new people? You may be an extrovert if you

Professor
Janet J. Taylor

recognize these characteristics in yourself. It can take time to determine your place on the personality spectrum. Everyone alternates between being more introverted and extroverted at different times.

Extraversion, extroversion, and introversion are concepts used to describe how people employ different attitudes to focus their energy. Renowned Swiss psychologist Carl Jung is credited as the pioneer of analytical psychology. Being an extrovert entails more than just being the life of the party, and shyness and introversion are not the same thing. Please learn more about extroverts' characteristics and how to identify whether you are one of them.

Professor
Janet J. Taylor

What Is an Extrovert?

Extroversion denotes a personality characteristic generally defined by expressive and outgoing patterns of conduct. Extroverts are typically warm, talkative, gregarious, and energetic. According to Jung, An extrovert gets energy from social interactions and the outside world. According to Jung, an extrovert may have an extroverted personality and experience excitement and ease in social situations. One could label an extrovert as a "people person," they would have a diverse group of pals to support this claim. It's typical for people to exhibit behavioral characteristics of both introverted and extroverted personality types; these individuals are known as ambiverts.

If you don't think you possess every trait associated with extroversion, remember that most people have a variety of personality types and rarely fit into one category. Personalities can shift throughout a lifetime, and you can discover that as

Professor
Janet J. Taylor

an adult, you've become more outgoing despite being shy as a youngster. Self-help books and therapy can even assist individuals in developing some degree of extroversion. What makes you distinctive are your personality qualities, which are frequently the result of a mix of growth, evolution, and heredity.

Professor
Janet J. Taylor

What Separates Introverts from Extroverts?

Knowing your personality type can help you enhance your relationships, find fresh approaches to challenges, and better understand your strengths and weaknesses. The most prevalent distinction between extroverts and introverts is that the former derive energy from social interactions with the outside world. In contrast, introverts are frequently more inward-focused and enjoy alone time.

The following are some typical distinctions between introverts' and extroverts' personalities:

Extroverts

- Tend to be described as enthusiastic
- Enjoy trying new things
- Enjoy working in groups

Professor
Janet J. Taylor

- Prefer to solve problems through conversation
- Are easy to make friends with
- Extroverts Can be impulsive

Introverts tend to be more reticent, enjoy time alone, prefer independent work, think things through carefully, and are naturally good listeners and creative thinkers.

In their engagement with others, introverts tend to be more reserved and process things best on their own. Extroverts have a wide social circle, are outgoing, and generally benefit from talking through things out loud. Certain traits of introversion, such as a preference for quietness, can help with stress and anxiety management. Conversely, extroverts who can function well in a team and are confident to take the initiative are frequently seen as capable and successful leaders.

Professor
Janet J. Taylor

Indices That May Point to an Extrovert

You're gregarious and enjoy meeting new people when you're out. If this describes you, you might ask yourself, "Am I an extrovert?" There are various methods to ascertain if you lean more toward introversion or extroversion, but measuring extroversion is not a precise science. One alternative is to take an online assessment such as the Myers-Briggs Type Indicator (MBTI), or you can think about extroverted personality qualities.

The following typical extroversion-related attributes can provide more understanding of your personality:

- Social contacts provide you with energy and encourage you after spending time with people.
- Excessive time spent by yourself depletes your vitality and might lead to a sluggish feeling.
- You enjoy being the center of attention and feel at ease in new circumstances.

Professor
Janet J. Taylor

- You enjoy striking up a conversation, even with strangers, and you frequently talk to sort through and arrange your thoughts.
- You frequently organize social gatherings and group excursions. You hardly ever decline an invitation to a social event or party.
- Your power lies in your ability to adapt, and you embrace making impromptu judgments in life.

It's not always easy to tell if you're an extrovert or an introvert. You might be more of an extrovert at work and feel at ease running a meeting, but you prefer to be alone at home. A person who possesses a combination of qualities is called an ambivert. Thinking inside yourself is the best way to find out what type of person you are. Think back on your individual experiences and preferences. Finding out what kind of person you are also helped by getting feedback from someone you feel comfortable with and trustworthy.

Professor
Janet J. Taylor

Benefits and Drawbacks of Being an Extrovert

- Being an extrovert has several advantages. Extroverts spend more time interacting with groups and are adept at forming social ties. More robust social skills will help you maintain friendships and increase your happiness. Another characteristic that unites extroverts and may help them succeed in jobs requiring a lot of communication is their capacity for topic discussion and expressiveness.

- Extroverts frequently struggle with long periods of seclusion and forget to consider their words before speaking. Extroverts may find listening more difficult because they are accustomed to taking over conversations in social situations.

Professor
Janet J. Taylor

- Extroverts and introverts both have advantages and disadvantages. Since they frequently get the best of both worlds, ambiverts might have the most significant benefit. However, by being conscious of the difficulties that come with your personality type, you may maximize your strengths and make wise adjustments.

Professor
Janet J. Taylor

Successful Techniques for Interacting with Extroverts

Working alongside extroverts can seem stressful and hectic to someone who leans introverted. It need not be, though. Effective business communication with extroverts appears like common sense once you know why extroverted behavior occurs. Due to basic biology, those who exhibit extroverted behavior may be more likely to communicate with others. Dopamine, a neurological substance, plays a vital function in the reward and pleasure centers of the brain, and extroverts have a more excellent dopamine response to reward than introverts. The prospect of reward energizes and motivates extroverts more when they engage with others.

Effective inter-office communication requires understanding how extroverted this heightened dopamine reaction fuels personalities. Extroverts are driven to take advantage of the many opportunities

Professor
Janet J. Taylor

for reward that arise during social encounters. Therefore, an extrovert will feel better if you make your interaction with them more rewarding. With that in mind, the following list of best practices for communication is sure to light up an extrovert's reward system and foster positive interpersonal interactions in the workplace and beyond.

STAY POSITIVE

Social settings usually pique the interest of extroverts more than introverts do. According to one study, people's photographs excited extroverts more than introverted participants, indicating that extroverts value social engagement more. Therefore, it shouldn't be shocking that an extrovert would feel let down when a social contact doesn't go as planned. In light of this, maintain constructive dialogue when speaking with an extrovert to build a solid professional rapport. Express gratitude for your time

Professor
Janet J. Taylor

with them; they will probably be eager to talk to you again.

PROVIDE A DANGER OR TROUBLE

Extroverts and high-stakes, high-reward situations are often complementary. Extroverts don't always see unpredictability negatively; instead, they see it as challenging. Extroverts had a higher neural response to surprise and favorable outcomes than introverts in an experiment including a gambling assignment. Present an assignment or project as an exciting chance or adventure to persuade an extrovert to take it on. Incorporating a small amount of risk is undoubtedly beneficial.

Professor
Janet J. Taylor

ALLOW THEM TIMES TO DISCUSS

Talking is what extroverts enjoy doing. You should avoid cutting an extrovert off when you are speaking with them. If you give them enough time to express what they want to say, they will leave you plenty of time to talk after they finish. If not, don't be afraid to express your desire to speak gently; extroverts are naturally drawn to various social situations and curious to hear what you say.

LEARN ABOUT THE INDIVIDUAL'S UNIQUENESS

The extrovert-introvert distinction is flawed because it views the two groups as distinct species. Extroverts and introverts are on a spectrum, with most of us falling somewhere around the middle. It's crucial to avoid assuming someone is introverted or extroverted when speaking with them. Instead, attempt to understand each person's distinct

Professor
Janet J. Taylor

inclinations, preferences, and emotional state during your engagement. Awareness is essential in all interactions.

Your outgoing coworkers can infuse the office with enthusiasm, originality, and honesty. By providing them with room to flourish and honoring their demands, you may enable your company to realize its most significant potential. Recall that the most creative, diverse companies welcome a wide range of individuals with various communication styles.

FIVE

Recognizing and Assessing Communication Styles

We may interact with others, share knowledge, and communicate our opinions. You engage with people constantly through fast texts or long coffee

Professor
Janet J. Taylor

conversations with friends. Much of your life is spent communicating, whether orally or nonverbally. However, our communication style is also shaped by who we are. Similar to how no two persons are identical, each has a communication style. You can interact and collaborate with others more effectively if you know certain communication styles and how to recognize them.

Professor
Janet J. Taylor

What are the 4 Types of Communication Styles?

There are numerous methods to characterize a person's communication style. Their communication method is one way. Southern New Hampshire University (SNHU) communication lecturer Dr. Daria S. LaFave suggests using these types to comprehend other people better. LaFave is not only an instructor but also a consultant for creating online courses and a researcher on topics like instructional design and developing relationships between teachers and students.

LaFave and other business executives assert that there are four primary forms of communication:

1. The absence of communication due to fear of speaking up is a common manifestation of passive communication; this could give rise to misconceptions.

Professor
Janet J. Taylor

2. Anger and judgment are often the driving forces behind aggressive communication, which can also lead to rigidity; this may make the atmosphere unfriendly.

3. Holding onto unpleasant emotions and allowing them to influence your behavior is known as passive-aggressive communication. It is an alternative to expressing your feelings honestly. Confusion and animosity may result from this.

4. While being confident, assertive communication still shows consideration for the opinions and feelings of others. Assertive communication fosters good interpersonal relationships and makes room for open dialogue.

Professor
Janet J. Taylor

What Other Elements Influence Someone's Communication Style?

Sorting communicators based on their styles can help understand people's behaviors or responses, but these approaches sometimes provide a partial picture.

"There are many facets to interpersonal communication," SNHU communication instructor Dr. Jim Owston stated. Owston thinks it's difficult to characterize a person by their communication style alone. It's only sometimes the case that someone who exhibits an aggressive communication style in a meeting does so regularly. Owston, who has over 30 years of experience as a teacher and 20 years of experience in broadcasting, identifies some crucial elements that he has observed affect communication, such as:

- Social and cultural norms
- Gender and roles in society
- Emotions and perception

Professor
Janet J. Taylor

- Environment or medium

These extra variables may explain the reasons for a person's communication style. However, they can also clarify how other people understand those messages. For instance, it's common knowledge that forceful communication skills are beneficial. A straightforward communicator who also shows consideration for the feelings and opinions of others is an assertive communicator.

"In some instances (though)," LaFave continued, "assertiveness can come across as aggression, which could have negative impacts on the person who is asserting themselves." One external aspect that might hurt how communication is interpreted is Gender, according to LaFave. Although men may be commended for their aggressiveness, the speaker stated that "women are more likely to be seen as aggressive when they assert themselves." It's critical to consider your communication style and the variables

Professor
Janet J. Taylor

that could influence your perception of another person's style.

Professor
Janet J. Taylor

How Can Communication Styles Be Recognized?

LaFave claims that knowing someone's communication style can benefit you in the following ways:

- Develop and communicate your message effectively
- Steer clear of or avert problems
- Accomplish your objectives
- Cultivate fruitful connections

However, how would one go about studying their style? The solution can require examining several variables.

Professor
Janet J. Taylor

1. Think About Your Partnership

A person's communication style may be influenced by their position or your connection with them.

Owston says, "It might help to identify that person's leadership style and traits if you are dealing with a superior."

However, it might be more beneficial to find out your romantic partner's love language if you're interested in understanding how they communicate. Owston believes building successful connections requires a solid understanding of someone's communication style. He advises knowing how your connection could affect how you interact with others. You can modify your strategy to fit that particular situation.

Professor
Janet J. Taylor

2. Make Use of Active Listening

One helpful tactic to determine someone's communication style is active listening.

"Active listening means listening not just with our ears but also with our eyes and heart," LaFave stated. "We can do that by asking questions that seek to understand the meaning behind what is being spoken." According to LaFave, listening actively also entails delaying making judgments.

Active listening can assist you in understanding the motivations behind a speaker's choice, for instance, if they are speaking clearly and succinctly. They may be pressed for time despite your assumption that they are hostile.

Different communication styles arise during an engagement, but it takes patience and time to identify the type accurately, according to LaFave.

Professor
Janet J. Taylor

3. Consider Emotional Intelligence

LaFave and Owston advise considering your and the other person's emotional intelligence levels while trying to understand someone else's communication style.

LaFave identifies five facets of emotional intelligence that may influence our modes of communication:

I. **Empathy:** The capacity to recognize and understand the feelings and experiences of another person by placing oneself in their position.

II. **Self-awareness:** The capacity to acknowledge your feelings, assets, and shortcomings and how they affect other people, as well as your ability to make decisions.

III. **Social skills:** Interacting with others to forge enduring and fulfilling bonds.

IV. **Self-regulation:** Under challenging circumstances, resist the want to let your destructive emotions win.

V. **Motivation:** Being aware of what drives your decision-making.

"The balance of these elements impacts our communication style," LaFave stated. "People who struggle with empathy or self-regulation may be more prone to communicate aggressively or passive-aggressively." According to LaFave's observations, individuals with more excellent proficiency in these domains typically possess elevated emotional intelligence, which leads to more effective interpersonal communication.

"Identifying a person's emotional intelligence will best help in understanding how and why a person communicates," Owston stated. "But understanding your emotional quotient will also aid in communicating with others."

Professor
Janet J. Taylor

What Influences Culture on Communication Styles?

Communication is heavily influenced by culture. Everybody brings unique values, beliefs, and experiences to a conversation. The U.S. Department of State claims that a person's communication style can be influenced by the significance that context has in their culture:

- **High-context communication:** This approach emphasizes formality, hierarchy, and relationships more than anything else. A person's communication style may change depending on the situation.
- **Low context communication:** This type is usually direct, intimate, and goal-oriented, with individuals expressing what they mean.

It can be perplexing when someone speaks in a way you're not used to. In certain circumstances, you

Professor
Janet J. Taylor

might not know how to react. Alternatively, you may need to see why someone would respond as you would to something that appeared natural.

"We all carry implicit biases that we may or may not be aware of," LaFave stated. "Before we even begin speaking, we form impressions of another person based on our initial observations, past experiences, and even biases that we may or may not be aware of."

Miscommunications and misconceptions can hamper strong relationships. Thus, it can be helpful to be aware that everyone communicates differently. Spend some time learning about the cultural communication norms of the person you are dealing with if they are from a different country or culture.

Professor
Janet J. Taylor

What Kinds of Communication Styles Exist in the Workplace?

Improving your communication skills is essential for both your personal and professional life. It's possible that your style at work blends in or diverges from your coworkers. "Someone with an aggressive communication style may come across as hostile and authoritarian, alienating others and creating a harmful work climate," LaFave stated. Yet, in other circumstances, a more assertive approach may be beneficial. According to her, an aggressive communicator can be ideal for a different project or company to maximize its time and resources.

A project may be impacted not only by a person's communication style but also by the clarity of their message.

"If instructions and the nature of the task are not clear to those (working on) the project, there will be problems," Owston stated. The project manager must convey

Professor
Janet J. Taylor

the objectives and results of the work clearly and concisely. One tool that can be useful in this approach is the SMART goal.

Uncertainty in communication can cause miscommunications and hold up the completion of activities. Everyone can work together more effectively and achieve good results with clear and explicit communication about roles and responsibilities.

Professor
Janet J. Taylor

What Influences Digital Environments on Communication Styles?

You could be accustomed to corresponding primarily through email or text messaging when you're online. You will likely need to tweak your online communication style to match your in-person manner.

According to Owston, "the main issue with digital communication is that it lacks significant nonverbal cues." Nonverbal cues can be seen in things like typing in all caps, underlining or bolding text, or using exclamation points excessively. All of them could be seen negatively. Readers can infuse their emotions and sentiments into your communication without nonverbal clues. If someone misinterprets your communication, what you meant to be assertive could come across as aggressive. To ensure that your message is understood clearly in an email or text message, pay attention to what you're writing and how you're writing it.

In Owston's words:

- Make thoughtful word choices.
- Steer clear of using the pronoun "you," as it suggests that the sender is criticizing the recipient.
- Sending messages by mistake can be prevented by typing them in a word processor.
- Make sure to verify all of your communications for spelling and grammar errors.

Owston suggests holding off on sending that SMS or email for a day if you plan to send something that could be misinterpreted or misinterpreted. "See if you have the same feeling you did the previous day," he stated. "You probably won't."

Professor
Janet J. Taylor

How Can Someone Get Better at Communicating?

While some people have it naturally, communication is a skill that can be developed with practice.

"The best way to improve our communication is to learn and to practice," LaFave stated. "It helps to set specific goals and work through them as we engage in everyday interactions."

Concentrating on your listening abilities is one strategy to enhance your communication abilities. "This might look like practicing active listening and trying to identify another question to ask about whatever is being discussed," LaFave stated. It can be a good idea to set the goal of deliberately answering rather than just reacting to what someone says. According to Owston, there are little things you can do each day to improve your communication

Professor
Janet J. Taylor

abilities. He advises anyone aiming to improve their communication skills to:

- Pose inquiries.
- Make conversations about the other person, not about you.
- Remember that how you phrase something matters more than the content.

Effective communicators are a crucial component of every winning team. Improving your communication abilities may involve more than just recognizing the communication styles of others; it may also involve self-reflection. By working to become a proficient communicator, you may strengthen your bonds with others, avoid misunderstandings, and gain a deeper understanding of them.

Professor
Janet J. Taylor

SIX

Identifying Lies in Others

Every human has the capacity for deception. And many of us do; according to several studies, Americans lie on average once or twice a day. Thankfully, professionals claim that there are techniques to recognize dishonesty. According to body language expert and author of How to Detect

Professor
Janet J. Taylor

Lies, Fraud, and Identity Theft: Field Guide Traci Brown, the first step in spotting a fib is establishing a baseline for how someone behaves when being truthful. Take note of how someone reacts, for instance, when asked a simple inquiry like, "Where are you from?" Their eyes go where? What is the sound of their voice?

Following establishing that baseline, Dr. Lillian Glass, author of The Body Language of Liars, suggests looking for changes in four distinct categories of behavior: body language, facial expressions, tone of voice, and speech content. She states, "Those are the codes of communication." Nevertheless, the indicators are not infallible; if an individual is uneasy in their chair, they can fidget, and if they are anxious, their voice might break.

According to Dr. Gary Brown, a certified family and marriage therapist located in Los Angeles, "There is debate within the healthcare community, and certainly in the area of mental health, about what are

Professor
Janet J. Taylor

reliable body language tips that can indicate that someone is lying." Dr. Jenny Taitz, a clinical psychologist in Los Angeles, adds that our perceptions may make it more difficult for us to understand the indications appropriately. "There are many reasons why someone could appear tense or uneasy, so it can be difficult to read someone by their body language accurately," the expert explains. For instance, it's simple to picture avoiding eye contact, which is frequently associated with lying, for various reasons, such as boredom, social anxiety, or embarrassment because you know you're lying. We sometimes read people better than we think we do. Nevertheless, there are specific cues that highly qualified body language specialists advise being aware of.

Professor
Janet J. Taylor

Body Language

The hands: According to Traci Brown, who has participated in an FBI deception training program and occasionally assists with investigations, liars typically make hand motions after they talk rather than during or before a conversation. She claims that "the mind is doing too many things, like making up the story, determining whether they are believed, and adding to the story accordingly." Thus, typical gestures that occur right before a sentence now happen after it.

The University of Michigan did a study in 2015 that examined 120 media clips of high-stakes court cases to compare the behavior of those who are lying against those who are telling the truth. According to the study, persons who lie are more likely than those who are telling the truth to make gestures with both hands; in 40% of the lying video, people did so, whereas in 25% of the truthful clips, they did so. In addition to turning their palms away from you, dishonest persons frequently do this, according to Traci Brown, a keynote speaker at financial institutions who assists them in identifying and preventing fraud. She claims it's an unintentional clue that they're suppressing feelings, information, or lying. "They might slide them under the table or put them in their pockets."

Itching and Fidgeting: According to Glass, who just finished a post-doctoral fellowship at UCLA focused on psychology and verbal and non-verbal communication, swaying the head sideways, rocking the body back and forth, or shuffling the feet can all be indicators of dishonesty. According to her, variations in the autonomic nervous system, which controls physiological processes, may also have an impact. According to her, nervousness can induce changes in the neurological system, leading to itchiness or tingling in the body and increased

Professor
Janet J. Taylor

Fidgeting. Similar findings were reached by UCLA psychology professor R. Edward Geiselman's research which showed that when people lie, they frequently engage in "grooming behaviors," including fiddling with their hair.

Expressions on the Face

The eyes: According to Glass, if someone is lying, they may stare or turn away at a pivotal point, which could indicate that they are shifting their eyes around to gather more information before speaking; this was supported by Geiselman's research at UCLA, which discovered that people occasionally glance away while lying. The University of Michigan's 2015 study also found that persons who lied were more likely to gaze than those who told the truth; in fact, 70% of the videos of people lying showed them staring right at the subjects of their deception.

Professor
Janet J. Taylor

However, there is still some disagreement on this. When someone is lying, the idea that people look in a certain way is refuted by a 2012 study published in Plos One. Even while reading too much into a person's demeanor is possible, Glass insists that some truth can be revealed by looking.

The Mouth: According to Traci Brown, rolling one's lips back until they nearly vanish may indicate deception by omission. "I've found that when people act that way, they're suppressing feelings or information," she claims. According to a UCLA study, those who lie are more inclined to lick their lips when confronted with delicate topics. According to Glass, pursed lips indicate a lack of interest in participating in the current discussion. She explains, "It's an instinctive reflex, meaning you don't want to speak."

Professor
Janet J. Taylor

Chestnut color shift: Have you ever seen someone turn ashen as a ghost while they talk? According to Glass, this could indicate dishonesty because it causes blood to surge out of the face.

Sweating or dryness: According to Glass, autonomic nervous system abnormalities can cause liars to sweat in the T-area of their faces (upper lip, forehead, chin, and surrounding the Mouth) or experience dryness in their Mouth and eyes. They may also lick or bite their lips, blink or squint excessively, or swallow forcefully.

Voice Tone

A high-pitched voice: According to Glass, anxious persons may have their vocal cord muscles constrict as a natural reaction to stress, which makes their voice seem incredibly high-pitched. There could be a grating in someone's voice as well. According to her, clearing one's throat as a coping mechanism for the soreness caused by the tense muscles can occasionally indicate dishonesty.

Abrupt volume shift: According to Glass, people who lie frequently raise their voices. She continues, "You'll get defensive sometimes, so you'll get louder."

Speech Content

Sayings like "let me tell you the truth," "honestly," or "I want to be honest with you" can be clues that someone is trying a bit too hard to persuade you of their honesty, according to Glass.

Using terms like "uh," "like," and "um": A University of Michigan study discovered that "speaking with more vocal fill" is frequently a sign of dishonesty.

Professor
Janet J. Taylor

According to Glass, people often use these expressions to give themselves extra time while considering what to say next.

Errors: According to Glass, most of us are not born liars. Thus, occasionally, we reveal the truth. Take note of statements such as "I was out to dinner with So-and-So — wait, I was working late" or "I was fired — no, wait, I mean I quit." She suggests you may have a liar on your hands.